# How to Write a ...p Proposal

## By
## Robert Villegas

How to Write a Sponsorship Proposal
By
Robert Villegas

Published by Document Services International

info@documentservicesinternational.com

www.documentservicesinternational.com

ISBN-13: 978-1517181642

ISBN-10: 151718164X

## Table of Contents

Dedicated to Steve Newey

## Introduction

Have you learned from experience that poorly produced sponsorship proposals lead to an under-funded team or business? If you have, this chapter from my book "Finding Sponsors" is for you. My goal is to provide you with some basic guidelines on what to communicate in order to produce a winning sponsorship proposal. These guidelines will focus on what you should be presenting to your potential sponsor to make the best business case for involvement with your team or entertainment company. I am assuming that you already know how to write effective business documents and do not need tips on how to write clear sentences and paragraphs.[1] If you have difficulty with the written word, you should seek out a competent professional writer.

Before you get started, you must understand that you are competing against the "Big Boys." They use professional printing companies, fancy folders, graphic designers, professional marketing writers, cloth letterhead paper and advanced computers and printers. They put their best foot forward to potential sponsors and know how to impress. They even use the power of trackside hospitality suites and Lear Jets. The good news is that you don't need to spend big bucks developing your sponsorship package and you can develop a proposal that looks professional. By putting some thought and effort into your proposal package you *can* compete effectively with the big boys. It

---

[1] My company helps sport and entertainment professionals write their sponsorship proposals. Check http://www.documentservicesinternational.com

doesn't have to cost more than the sponsorship dollars you need and you don't need to hire a consultant who costs more than the team.

I've seen a number of sponsorship proposals that say, in effect, "I will do my absolute best to promote my sponsors," as if an intention of that type is going to bring attention to the offer. Such a statement is a giveaway that the driver or team doesn't have a clue about how to promote sponsors. "Thanks but no thanks." The people looking at your proposal are trained professional marketing people who know, for the most part, how to get the most from their marketing programs. They look for professionalism and marketing savvy in the teams they bring on, not just a statement of intentions. This means that if you are going to be successful, your proposal must look like and speak the language of the "Big Boys."

This chapter is written with the small-budget race team in mind. However, the ideas presented here can benefit any sports team and entertainment group including the big-budget organization. Most of these guidelines were developed out of my own efforts to write effective sponsorship proposals for clients.

## Before You Start

Before you start writing your sponsorship proposal, you must set a goal for your document. First, decide how much you will need in order to accomplish your goals. The old Penske axiom applies here: "Speed costs money – how fast do you want to go?" This is your money goal and you should make sure it is an adequate amount. Secondly, you should include in your money goal enough for the time and effort it will take to deliver on the benefits you promise your sponsors. Remember, sponsors are not going to go away once they write the check. They are going to come around to bask in the glory...they expect to be treated well and they want lunch and premium tickets – free. So include these costs as well...and while you are at it, consider money for the people who will do the work of schmoozing the sponsors. They must be paid.

Another key issue before you start is to identify each sponsor's expectations for a sponsorship proposal. Active major sponsors will often produce "sponsorship guidelines" that communicate to teams what they expect to see in the proposal. You should ask specifically if they have such guidelines before you even begin putting something together for them. If they don't have guidelines, here are some important questions to ask your potential sponsor:

- Is our form of sport or entertainment a category of sponsorship you favor? If the answer is "No," then inquire about the reason for that. If the reason appears insurmountable, ask what it would take for them to change their mind. Too much resistance here is an indication that you should move on to another potential sponsor. If the resistance is minimal and there is a chance that they would change their minds, then ask if you can include an argument on this in your presentation to them.

- Do you require exclusivity in your industry category? This means, if they are a beer company, they don't want another beer manufacturer on the car or at the event. You will waste your time presenting a proposal if you already have a sponsor competing with them in their industry.
- What is your primary goal in sponsorship and what do you expect your sponsored teams or entertainment partners to include in their proposal?
- Do you require any audience statistical reporting, research or other sales activities at the track or venue?
- Do you look for a certain percentage of the sponsorship investment to be spent by the team on enhancing the sponsorship?
- How much do you usually spend, in addition to the sponsorship investment, in leveraging the sponsorship and what would you like the team to do to support these expenditures? This can be measured in dollars or in a percentage of the cost of the sponsorship (Typically, a sponsor won't get their money's worth unless they spend an equal amount to the amount spent on the sponsorship in leveraging it with additional promotion programs).

- What are your core branding goals? What tag lines, images, icons, values and messages do you seek to promote through sponsorship and how can we aid you in communicating them?
- What kind of cross-promotional strategies have you successfully pursued in the past?

Needless to say, the value of having these questions answered before the preparation of the sponsorship proposal is crucial to the success of your proposal document. A key point to remember, the success of your proposal will depend on how thorough you are in gathering information about your potential sponsor. Most of the time, you won't be able to get this information without their assistance.

## Develop Your Sponsorship Inventory

Most companies work hard to develop an inventory of promotional programs and opportunities in order to implement their marketing strategies. You should do the same for your organization and for your sponsors. This inventory is basically your little black bag of things that you can do for a sponsor and you should have them on the tip of your tongue at all times. You've already done a lot of work in this area with your Sponsorship Sales Matrix. Now is the time to put that work to use for your proposal. Below are some suggestions on what you can offer your sponsors. These are just a starting point. If you have other ideas, don't hesitate to offer them to your sponsors.

- Preferred Supplier Status – this status tells the public that you use only this sponsor's products because of your loyalty and their quality.
- Naming Rights – the sponsor purchases the right to change the name of your team or organization so it is no longer the name you gave it but the sponsor's name.
- Official Product Status – similar to Preferred Supplier Status except that you have designated your sponsor as your "official" supplier – this status is most often used for major events like the Super Bowl or Indy 500 or NASCAR, but if your team garners enough attention, you can do it as well.
- Single Event Sponsor – some sponsors are more interested in a particular market – you can sell them

primary sponsorship while you compete or entertain in that market alone – needless to say, you'll need to work it out with your other sponsors.

- Primary Sponsor – this is the sponsor that obtains primary signage positioning most visible to the public - the primary sponsor provides the biggest share of your budget.
- Secondary Sponsor – the company that purchases a secondary sponsorship obtains logo and/or signage placement visible to the public much smaller than that of the primary sponsor
- Affiliate Sponsor – this company has purchased a smaller signage position or has traded products or services in return for that placement.
- In-car Camera Sponsorship – When the television camera looks out through your in-car camera, you want this company's logo visible in the camera shot. Additional camera ideas include GoPro cameras on athletes and entertainers during events and other promotions where logos are visible.
- Category exclusivity – this means the sponsor gains exclusive status in a particular industry or product category – they are your only sponsor among their competitors.
- Licensing – this enables the sponsor to be the sole licensee for any products that relate to your team, t-shirts, posters, die cast cars, etc.
- Endorsements – this is a specific category of opportunity where your team, driver or celebrity endorses a particular product to the public in return for dollars.

- Cross-promotional sponsorship – this is where one of your sponsors gives you product instead of dollars – you take the product and negotiate with another sponsor for special shelf space positioning and advertising in a retail location – then you receive a percentage of the profits from the retailer.

## Modular Proposal Sections

The modular proposal document approach has been used successfully by many companies. "Document reuse" means better sponsorship messages that have been tested and proven to work over time. By creating each section of your proposal as a separate module, using the heading as a title for the module, you can edit those that need to be tailored to a particular prospect's proposal guidelines and their specific needs while the rest of the document stays consistent. I recommend the modular approach as a cost-effective strategy. By keeping a menu of sponsorship proposal modules you save time and money and ensure your message gets across consistently.

However, there can be problems with document reuse. You must ensure that you read the entire document thoroughly once you have put the pieces together. Make sure you then edit if necessary. Ensure you haven't left in the document the names of other companies and individual's names. And you should make sure you check the document for consistency of message to eliminate any contradictions you may have created while editing one module and keeping the others the same. Always, always, always check and recheck. Every writer needs an editor.

## How Does Your Proposal Look?

Let's face it, the "big boys" know how to create attractive proposals. You must ensure that yours is at least as well written and speaks the right marketing language. A neat looking document that presents its subject in a clear and concise manner will get attention regardless of whether it comes in a pretty package. If you struggle with the written word, don't hesitate to ask those around you for editorial and grammatical advice. You don't want to spoil your chances because of a misspelled word or poorly written prose.

Yet with today's computer technologies, color printers and word processing software, it is possible to format your document so it is appealing. If you are not good with computers, ask someone around you to help in formatting and organizing it for you. Just remember, the important issue is whether it is clearly written, well organized and communicates well the benefits of your sponsorship packages. Pay attention to the details of what you are communicating and you will take a big step toward earning sponsorship.

An excellent resource is your local UPS Store or Kinko's. This company has state-of-the-art computers and printers. They can even consult with you on how to make your document attractive, how to properly bind it, cover it and ship it. Take advantage of this low-cost resource for upgrading the quality of your documents.

## The Parts of a Sponsorship Proposal

The elements of a great sponsorship proposal are:

### Executive Summary

Although the Executive Summary appears first, you should write it last. The Executive Summary is the Introduction to the proposal and should spell out, in briefest terms, the offer that will be presented in more detail in the rest of the document. You should provide an overview of what is to come so the reader's mind is set about what is to come. It should provide a succinct description of the advantages of developing a partnership with your organization and a brief statement of your commitment to ensuring their investment is well-spent.

You should think of the Executive Summary as an effort to sell the sponsor without his/her having to read the rest of the document. You should express, in briefest terms, the best business case, the most important reasons why the potential sponsor should continue reading.

The Executive Summary should contain:
- A brief introduction to the sponsorship offer
- A brief introduction to the organization and the key personalities
- A short statement of sponsorship benefits
- A statement of your marketing experience and commitment
- The best business case for accepting your sponsorship

offer in terms of tangible, bottom line benefits.

Sample Executive Summary

When Johnny Kennedy was five years old, his dad took him to the Long Beach Grand Prix to see Champ Car star Paul Tracy, who young Johnny had begun to idolize as his favorite driver.

His dad was able to flag Tracy down and asked if he would speak to Johnny. Tracy, one of the biggest names in racing at the time, agreed and spent several minutes with the wide-eyed youngster. From that day forward, Johnny became a race car driver.

After eleven years of preparation, Johnny Kennedy is ready to take the next step in his racing career. For 2017, Johnny has signed with Ma-Con Motorsports to race the ADAC Formula Masters series in Europe. At the age of 17, Johnny is one of the rising stars in American road racing and is a consistent winner and top competitor. Realizing that talent in the car is only part of the success of a modern professional driver, Johnny has been described by Motor Trend as a driver who "gets it". He is mature, poised and media savvy.

Johnny has been featured on SPEED TV, "In the Pits" radio shows (he will be a regular feature in 2017), Motortrend.com, Motorsports.com, European Car magazine and Microsoft TV ads. Johnny has also signed to do "In the Pits" radio show in Washington, D.C. where he will be a regular as a European correspondent for the series.  He is a well-rounded driver who is also an A-B grade home-schooled student in his junior year of high school. And it's no secret that Johnny Kennedy is poised to make a strong challenge in the ADAC series.

Based in Sterling, VA Johnny has worked to create excellent promotional programs that mean terrific sales power for his sponsors. Whether you seek to increase brand loyalty, create more visibility, change or reinforce your image, drive retail traffic, stimulate sales or entertain clients, Johnny will work to help you achieve any or all of these objectives.  He will perform, not only on the track, but off the track as well.

## Team/Company Introduction

Put your best foot forward. Include accomplishments, personal bios, and lots of pictures of your key personalities, the business office, anything that will reflect your organization's dynamic character. This section is a critical component and you must ensure that everything here is positive and energetic. Include your mission statement and your basic philosophy.  What special capabilities does the team/company have that gives it a competitive marketing edge and how do you approach your relationship with sponsors? How long have you been in business and who are the owners and managers?

If the bulk of your operating budget is set, it might be helpful for the sponsor to be informed about the situation in general terms. In other words, if 70% of your budget has been raised, let the sponsor know that his/her support could make a world of difference. This issue might convince them that the program is strong and viable. You might want to indicate which other sponsors are involved with your program so they can understand how they might fit in with your program. Keep in mind, before they even think about giving you money, you'll have to go through a due diligence process regarding your financial status. So if you cannot function without this sponsor, let them know how much their participation means to the future plans of the team. Let them know how long you've been in business and some of your accomplishments over the years. This could be critical for you. Be careful not to shed a too negative light on this as it might cause them to balk, but if handled properly, they will understand your situation and look more toward the benefits they might gain by helping you out.

Team Introduction should include:
- Team accomplishments
- Major team personalities
- Short history of the team
- Mission statement
- Special competitive advantages
- Team situation (financial)
- Some major sponsors

## Team/Athlete Record

Create tables and graphs that highlight your past successes. This is your chance to prove to the sponsor that you can provide logo impressions that get noticed and television time and/or victories and top three finishes can all show what you can bring to the sponsor. If you've had a stellar record, then talk about how many people have seen you perform or win or battle for the lead. Give statistics and show value. If you are an up-and-comer without a distinguished record, talk about your goals and aspirations and your need of a viable sponsor that can bring you to the front. You must spin this section in as many ways as possible to present yourself as a winner, a record setter, a striver or a hard driver that gets attention.

Team Record should include:
- Overview of major accomplishments
- Goals and aspirations of the team
- Statistics on television time earned.

Sample Driver/Athlete Record

Auto Racing Accomplishments

2016: Formula Renault 1600 – 12 podiums, 1 win and Gatorz Eyewear Hard Charger Award, 4th in Championship

2017: Formula Renault 2000 – 12 podiums, 3 wins and Gatorz Eyewear Hard Charger Award, 4th in Championship

2018 VW Jetta TDI – 4 podiums, 2 wins, 2<sup>nd</sup> place in Championship

## Driver/Celebrity Introduction

This is where the sponsor meets the key personalities of your team/organization. Show the personalities at their best with nice pictures, smiling, signing autographs, driving with two wheels in the air (but still under control), singing to a huge audience, acting on stage, etc. Talk about his/her family life, spouse, children, father, mother, etc. Give him/her a human touch and don't just mention success in the venue but also in the boardroom (if any) or performing charitable activities, etc. If he isn't a star, make him one.

Be upfront with the sponsor and let them know whether the celebrity is signed or pending sponsorship. How long will his/her contract be in effect and where will he compete or perform?

Driver/Celebrity Introduction should include:
- Biography
- Accomplishments
- Special issues and characteristics of the driver/athlete/celebrity from a marketing/personality perspective

Sample Driver Bio

- Born: 17 January 1992, Simi Valley, CA

- Home: Sterling, VA
- Raised: Las Vegas, NV
- Years racing: 11
- Career goal: Formula 1 and win Le Mans before 21 years of age.
- Racing Heroes: Fernando Alonso, Takuma Sato, Colin McRae, Steve McQueen.
- Education highlights: GATE (2001-2002), Nevada State Finalist NASA Contour Outreach program, currently in a university accredited homeschool program.

For someone who's only 17, Johnny Kennedy certainly does not act his age. The composed, articulate and confident teenager has his sights set on Formula 1 and what he calls the ultimate test of man and machine. He is determined to win the 24 Hours of Le Mans before being old enough to drink the victory champagne at 21.

Johnny and his family, who now live in Virginia, have been hard at it for years and sacrificed much - no boat, fancy car, lots of travel and long hours - to follow the dream. The 2017 ADAC Formula Masters series is yet another step up the motorsports ladder for Johnny, who has already taken several. His first big time racing experience was in the Snap-On Stars of Karting series that was founded by IRL star Bryan Herta.

## Marketing Opportunities

Sponsors expect you to have answers for their business marketing needs. They are not just along for the ride. They want to sell, impress and excite the fans. After all, this is show business and you must put on a good show so you are noticed – and when you are, the sponsor is also noticed. In this section, let the sponsor know, with as much specificity as
possible, what you can do to make them noticed, to get logo or product impressions. Count it all and be creative. Make sure your preproposal informs the potential sponsor about the highest number of impressions (and to which market) that you will generate.

However, your programs should include more than just logo impressions. There are a number of things you can do to showcase the driver/celebrity and sponsors. Your key personalities must be available and ready to meet, speak, show, talk, present, promote and educate. In this section, you should detail just what the driver will do for the sponsor, the kinds of things he/she has done for other sponsors in the past and how many times he will do it for this sponsor.

Ever wonder why the most successful drivers and athletes have the most in sponsorship dollars? Certainly, they were winners from the beginning, but more importantly they do things for the sponsors. Let's face it, the celebrity who gets out front for the sponsors is the best bet for getting sponsorship dollars. Communicate your celebrity's accessibility and willingness. If he has a marketing degree, that's even better.

Don't forget other opportunities. Look at what the most successful teams and organizations do and take a lesson.

There are opportunities for hospitality and entertaining sponsor customers and prospects, cross selling between sponsors, up selling at retail outlets, promotional product packages that feature the team and driver and a host of other creative things you can do that will mean a winning proposal. Let the sponsor know that you are marketing savvy and that you are capable of ensuring their marketing success. Above all, don't just say, "I'll do whatever it takes." That's an amateur. Show them that you know how to do it.

Marketing Opportunities section should include:
- Marketing opportunities
- Overview of team/company approach for marketing sponsor products/services
- Marketing commitments
- Special marketing benefits that derive from you alone

Sample Marketing Opportunities

Johnny Kennedy specializes in capturing the excitement of yacht racing by achieving individual and team goals that will impact and deliver your message to your target audience. Johnny can custom-design and execute a program to meet your needs for successfully marketing your company, products, services and/or events.

Below you will find Johnny's sponsorship program offerings. This section details his programs and how he can work with you to create a program tailored to your specific marketing goals. The Basic Program is a turn-key package which includes the following:

- The Vendee Globe Yacht Race
- Experienced team of professionals to prepare and maintain the yacht and race equipment
- Sponsor benefits packages
- Current configuration, race prepared 60 Foot Open Racing Yacht

The Vendee Globe Yacht Race has a strong content appeal. This race is a major global platform for promotion. The Vendee Globe Yacht Race is a true global media story that is not attached to a traditional marketing vehicle.

Publicity-Driven Events include the following:
- PR Campaign targeting magazine, website and TV program outlets
- Local PR targeting radio, print and TV
- Media generated events around the world
- Online media events – live webcast events

As a sponsor for Johnny Kennedy, you gain the ability to use yacht racing to promote your brands, logos and products for a fraction of the cost of conventional advertising. Opportunities exist to use the significant marketing power of the Vendee Globe Yacht Race in television, radio, Internet and mail promotions to further enhance your sponsorship investment in a way targeted to your customer.

Once, we agree upon a sponsorship package, we will work with you to carefully plan and execute all promotional activities that you'd like to implement.  As a sponsor, you will receive first class treatment at every event you attend.  Johnny Kennedy will be on hand to ensure the experience is first-rate and memorable for you, your employees and your clients.  Special events can be coordinated for an additional fee and we can put you in touch with the right people at the sanctioning body corporate office to make them happen.  Every service we provide will be closely managed by a key member of the team staff who will be responsible for ensuring your expectations are met.

At strategic points in the competition, a team manager will call you to let you know how things are going.  We will prepare special information releases to inform you and company officers of the successes Johnny has achieved in the competition.  You will receive an estimate of how many people were exposed to your logo.  We will tell you of any special exposure you received, leads and/or marketing information obtained, interviews granted and how many times we were able to get you mentioned on camera or on the air.

Sports and racing sites are among the most popular on

the Internet. Sponsors' websites receive the benefit of links from the team website that is certain to receive thousands of hits as the team becomes better known and the fan base grows. Consider how you can use the race to create valuable web content, e.g. educational programs that would enhance the sponsors reach. In addition, the sanctioning organization's website will receive thousands of hits daily and will l nk to the team's site giving you additional exposure. We can also develop special web promotions and contests to further promote your company.

## Sponsorship Packages

Here is where you put the nuts and bolts of your proposal together. Remember, the goal we talked about before: the number of dollars you need to be successful. Now it is time to translate this goal to a set of sponsorship offerings.

Take a look at your Sponsorship Sales Matrix and identify the programs and other sponsorship offerings you think the prospect is looking for. In your investigating phase you should have gotten lots of information about their marketing goals, branding strategies and promotional programs. Use this information to prove to the sponsor that your packages will meet their needs better than those of your competitors.

First of all, each offering should have a name that sells it, distinguishes it from other offerings. If you want to call it "Primary Sponsor" or "Title Sponsor" that is fine, but ensure that it has a name that conveys prestige and separateness from the other offerings. Also ensure that the offerings are easy to understand so there is little doubt about what the offering will do for the sponsor. Be creative and set yourself apart with some winning titles. Even those offerings that involve small dollar contributions, sometimes called "affiliate sponsors" should invoke some sort of prestige. Otherwise, how could you sell it?

Each offering should have a set of "benefits" that go to the sponsor in return for the dollars. This is where the sponsor can see the strengths that you bring. Ensure that the benefits respect the amount contributed for each program. Don't give a lower paying sponsor something you don't also give the higher paying sponsor. In other words, if they pay more, they should know they are getting more.

Use the "Features and Benefits" approach. A feature is a characteristic about the offering that brings about a benefit to the purchaser. A features and benefits statement goes like this: "Because of <feature> you receive <benefit>." An example: "A primary sponsor receives larger logo placement on the race car, transporter and team uniforms. This means your logo or product will be seen by more potential customers."

A knowledge-based qualifier for this statement would be "Statistics (cite the source of the data) prove that race team and driver fans are XX% more likely to reward the primary sponsor when it comes to purchasing your product category." Then the "clincher" statement would be: "In addition, we will do X, Y and Z to ensure even more fans see the primary sponsor logo multiplying by a factor of X the amount of exposure you receive."

The following are almost staples in sponsorship packages:

- The sponsor's name will appear in all materials, letterheads and literature created by the team
- The manager and driver/s agree to make a certain number of appearances for the sponsor with expenses paid by the sponsor
- The sponsor's name is included in all press releases
- Team members agree to wear the sponsor's lapel pin or baseball cap at all times
- Team agrees to distribute sponsor's business cards and sales literature at all events where possible

Offer assistance with other types of promotions in which the sponsor might be interested such as series sponsorship programs, race title sponsorship, official product provider status, track or arena signage, etc. Sweeten the pot by asking for additional dollars if you win a number of races, set track records, sit on the pole, etc. in order to motivate the team and driver to strive harder. Benefits could be special announcements and press and television coverage when the incentive is achieved.

Make sure that there is some exclusivity of benefits for the higher value packages and be clear about this so there is no confusion. You should also indicate your policies regarding non-compatible sponsors (or direct competitors) as well as the sponsor's right of review regarding these relationships.

Your sponsorship packages should include
- Sponsorship package names
- Sponsorship package features and benefits
- Package prices

**Package Prices**

After you describe each sponsorship package or offering, you want to indicate the price of each package. You can do it after the description of each package or in a separate table in this section. I prefer the price to be the last item mentioned after the description but a nice table detailing the package name and price is also easy to review and understand. Always scale the table with the most expensive package listed first and then the rest in ascending order.

Package Prices should include:
- A table of sponsor packages with the benefits of each linked to the price for each package

Sample Packages and Prices Table

**Sponsorship Benefits – Primary Partner**

**Visual Identification**
The Primary Partner's corporate identity will receive exclusive exposure on the:
**RACE CAR and uniform – Only one Primary Sponsor on the car – car and uniform can be designed in the corporate colors of the sponsor.**

**OTHER APPLICATIONS**
—    pit equipment and pit wall signage (where possible)
—    hero/autograph cards

**Formal Designation**
Your company can use the designation of Primary Partner or Primary Sponsor.

**Press and Publication Billing**
An initial press release will be issued about the partnership agreement to all major publications and news services. All subsequent press releases during the race event will include the Primary Partner's name. Placement of the partner's identity on Johnny Kennedy Motorsports web site with a short description and link to the partner's web site.

**VIP Passes and Hospitality**
Guest passes will be provided for each race event based upon rules at the event. Each pass provides the holder with full access to the racing facility and designated

hospitality area as established by the series when appropriate. On certain days, any of your staff, customers or clients can enjoy a tour of the paddock.

**Advertising and Merchandising**
Use of the Primary Partner designation in trade advertising and on promotional material leading up to and after each race event. Casual wear can be developed for the partner to use for their own promotional activities and can be negotiated.

**Endorsements and Personal Services**
The right to use the driver and team logos, their names, likeness and identification in advertising and promotional material leading up to and after each race event. Use of the driver's personal time as a product or service endorser, consultant and spokesperson leading up to and after the race event. Personal appearances will be negotiated to avoid conflicts with team events and other commitments.

**First Option Continued Partnership Opportunity**
Every Primary Partner will have the first option of continuing their business relationship with Johnny Kennedy Motorsports in 2019 and beyond.

## Sponsorship Benefits – Secondary Partners

### Visual Identification
The Secondary Partner's corporate identity will receive exposure commensurate with level of financial investment (see color chart above) and will have the exclusive logo exposure on the:

### RACE CAR and Uniform
— Secondary logos and brands as indicated by color charts

### OTHER APPLICATIONS
— hero/autograph cards
— pit equipment (where possible)

### Formal Designation
Your company can use the designation of Secondary Partner or Secondary Sponsor

### Press and Publication Billing
An initial press release will be issued about the partnership agreement to all major publications and news services. All subsequent press releases during the race event will include the Secondary Partner's name where appropriate and consistent with the release. Placement of the partner's identity on Johnny Kennedy Motorsports website with a short description and link to the partner's web site.

### VIP Passes and Hospitality
Guest passes will be provided for each race event. Each

pass provides the holder with full access to the paddock racing facility and the designated hospitality area. On designated days, the opportunity exists to have any of your staff, customers or clients enjoy a tour of the paddock. Number of passes is commensurate with the level of investment. Some investments do not qualify.

**Advertising and Merchandising**
Use of the Secondary Partner designation in trade advertising and on promotional material leading up to and after the race event. Casual wear can be developed for the partner to use for their own promotional activities and can be negotiated.

**Endorsements and Personal Services**
The right to use the driver and team logos, their names, likeness and identification in advertising and on promotional material leading up to and after each race event. Use of the driver's personal time as a product or service endorser, consultant and spokesperson leading up to and after each race event. Personal appearances will be negotiated on an individual basis to avoid conflicts with team events, other commitments and Primary sponsor conflicts. The level of service is commensurate with the level of investment.

**First Option Continued Partnership Opportunity**
Every Secondary Partner will have the first option of continuing and/or escalating their business relationship with Johnny Kennedy Motorsports in 2018 and beyond.

## Sponsorship Benefits – Associate Partners

### Visual Identification
The Associate Partner's corporate identity will receive exposure commensurate with level of financial investment (see color chart above) and will have the exclusive logo exposure on the:

### RACE CAR and Uniform
— associate logos and brands as indicated by color charts
—

### OTHER APPLICATIONS
— pit equipment (where possible)
— hero/autograph cards
—

### Formal Designation
Your company can use the designation of Associate Partner or Associate Sponsor


### Press and Publication Billing
An initial press release will be issued about the partnership agreement to all major publications and news services. All subsequent press releases during the race event will include the Associate Partner's name where appropriate and consistent with the release. Placement of the partner's identity on Johnny Kennedy Motorsports website with a short description and link to the partner's web site.


### VIP Passes and Hospitality
Guest passes will be provided for each race event. Each pass provides the holder with full access to the paddock

racing facility and the designated hospitality area. On designated days, the opportunity exists to have any of your staff, customers or clients enjoy a tour of the paddock. Number of passes is commensurate with the level of investment. Some investments do not qualify.

## Advertising and Merchandising
Use of the Associate Partner designation in trade advertising and on promotional material leading up to and after the race event. The possibility of team gear and casual wear being made available for the partner to use for their own promotional activities can be negotiated.

## Endorsements and Personal Services
The right to use the driver and team logos, their names, likeness and identification in advertising and on promotional material leading up to and after each race event. Use of the driver's personal time as a product or service endorser, consultant and spokesperson leading up to and after each race event. Personal appearances will be negotiated on an individual basis to avoid conflicts with team events, other commitments and Primary sponsor conflicts. The level of service is commensurate with the level of investment.

## First Option Continued Partnership Opportunity
Every Associate Partner will have the first option of continuing and/or escalating their business relationship with Johnny Kennedy Motorsports in 2018 and beyond.

## Recommended Programs

If you are tailoring the proposal for a particular sponsor prospect, you may want to emphasize a specific program with the explanation that this will ensure the best result for their particular needs. Always leave yourself an out by suggesting that the prospect can still select other options or even combinations of options. Offer them long-term savings if they sign a multi-year contract and additional benefits.

Sample Recommended Programs

As a sponsor for Johnny Kennedy Motorsports, you gain the ability to use your motor sports involvement to promote your brands, logos and products for a fraction of the cost of conventional advertising. Opportunities exist to use the marketing power of the European-based ADAC Formula Masters Series in television, radio, Internet, mail and on track promotions to further enhance your sponsorship investment in a way targeted to your customer. In addition, because Johnny is based in the U.S. there is a bonus of exposure in the U.S. media via internet, radio and print channels. Partnering with Johnny provides a global presence for a modest investment in 2017.

In addition, we will work with you to ensure additional exposure including autograph and speaking appearances by Johnny Kennedy, event tickets, special promotions and on-track meetings with your clients and employees. Got something special in mind? Just ask and we'll do our best to help make it happen. Let's talk about additional ways we can get your logos or brands exposed.

**Activation Plan**
This is probably the most important part of your proposal because it communicates to the potential sponsor that you know how to deliver a winning marketing partnership. You must ensure that the sponsor **knows** you can deliver.

A brief description of how you plan on implementing and ensuring that the sponsor gets the maximum benefit for his investment will ensure the sponsor that you've been there and you know you can deliver. You may want to introduce him to the people who will manage the sponsorship at each event and you want to indicate, to some degree, what will be done in specific markets that the customer considers key.

Activation Plan should include:
• What will be done for the sponsor
• Who will do it
• When will it be done
• Where it will be done

Sample Activation Plan

Once, we agree upon a sponsorship package, we will work with you to carefully plan and execute all promotional activities that you'd like to implement on and off the track. As a sponsor, you will receive first class treatment at every event you attend. Team members and the team owner will be on hand to ensure the trackside experience is first-rate and memorable for you, your employees and your clients. Special events can be coordinated for an additional fee and we can put you in touch with the right people at the series corporate office to make them happen. Every service we provide will be closely managed by a key member of the team staff who will be responsible for ensuring your expectations are met.

## Reporting and ROI

In this part of the proposal, you should communicate how you plan on reporting your activities to the sponsor. Let them know what your communication plan will be and what you will be communicating. This will ensure the sponsor that you view yourself as a valuable partner and employee who is committed to their success. Indicate who their contact person will be, introduce that person and their qualifications for the job. How often will you be reporting to the press and media and will you provide a press clipping service[2] for the sponsor. What other series stats and published reports will you be providing and how often?

If the news isn't good, then be honest and ask the sponsor if you can meet with him or her to develop a new strategy. This strategy will help you keep tabs on what the sponsor is thinking and show your willingness to work

---

[2] A term designating an effort to provide articles clipped from the newspaper about the sponsor, team, athlete or celebrity that mention the sponsor. This could also include Internet articles and media as well.

with him to ensure you can make a positive contribution to his success.

Sample Reporting and ROI

At Johnny Kennedy Motorsports, we are dedicated to ROI for our sponsors. We are seeking long-term relationships and will do all we can to promote our sponsors at every event. Toward this goal, we have developed business processes and procedures to ensure that you obtain maximum exposure. Our on-track team of marketing specialists is trained to actively pursue our sponsors' interests. We will engage in promotional programs, literature handouts, product giveaways and lead development activities. We will also work with you to develop data gathering programs such as surveys, contests and additional programs so you can obtain names and addresses of willing customers. Please note: the level and extent of such programs are dependent upon the level of sponsorship investment. We can negotiate promotions outside the original sponsorship agreement for a fee.

Also, after each event, a team manager will call you to let you know how things went. We will prepare a special information release to inform you and company officers of the significant successes we achieved. You will receive a report on how many times we went around the track and an estimate of how many people were exposed to your logo. We will tell you of any special exposure you received, leads and/or marketing information obtained, interviews granted and how many times we were able to get you mentioned on camera or on the air.

Sample Website Promotions

Sports and racing sites are among the most popular on the Internet. In addition, the Internet medium has become a major promotional tool because of its open architecture and worldwide scope. Sponsors' websites receive the benefit of links from the Johnny Kennedy Motorsports website that is certain to receive thousands of hits as the driver becomes better known and as his fan base grows. Fans will visit the site to learn about him, his results and to see pictures of him on the track and in the pits – all of which expose sponsor logos. Because of additional site promotions, search engine optimization, Google listings, links on Johnny's site to your site and contests to further promote your company (subject to negotiation) site stats and rankings will get a boost. Finally, we will promote sponsor websites at the track through literature handouts, hero cards and on the race car.

## Contact Information

If you are going to be emailing your proposal to potential sponsors in an effort to obtain interest, make sure you include contact information so they know who to contact in the event they would like to pursue a meeting. You can also include your mailing address and website here if you like. Don't forget your twitter and Facebook handles if you'd like to include them.

## Optional Sections

## Past Performance References

If you have a history of performing well for your sponsors, you may want to enlist those past or present sponsors as references. This option could make a huge difference if your existing sponsors are happy with the return on their investment and they may be willing to praise you to another potential sponsor. This may even help your sponsors develop additional business opportunities among themselves as well. Be careful, however that you don't use a competitor of your potential sponsor as this will certainly ruin the deal.

Make sure you coach your sponsors on what to say and how to say it. Again, before you provide a reference, make sure your sponsors are enthusiastic about the results you have
given them.

## Fan Demographics and Race/Event Schedule

Demographic data reveals the makeup of the fan base that attends your events. Characteristics such as income level, age, marital status, education, occupation and lifestyle are analysed by sponsors to determine if your fans are a good fit for their

products and services. It is important to the sponsor that the fan base for your events (including both spectators at venue and those watching on television) has significant shared characteristics with their target customers.

You should be able to find good demographic data from sanctioning bodies or by taking a survey at events. Most sport sanctioning bodies have conducted their own surveys and are willing to provide the information if it helps you obtain sponsorship.

If you know that your fan demographics are a good match for this sponsor, then mention this fact in the Executive Summary and put some charts or statistics in the appendix. This will give the potential sponsor a good feel for the series makeup and whether it appeals to target customers. Play this up if the match is good and handle it carefully if the match is not. For instance, if the major market for a sponsor includes mostly women, perhaps you don't want to emphasize the fact that 80% of your series fans are men. But do mention that many men come to the track or watch on television with their wives or girlfriends.

An event schedule enables the sponsor to determine if

you participate in events within key markets for the company. If you are aware of their key markets, make sure you mention that in your Executive Summary and you may want to offer special activities in those markets to give your sponsor additional exposure.

Sample Demographic Charts

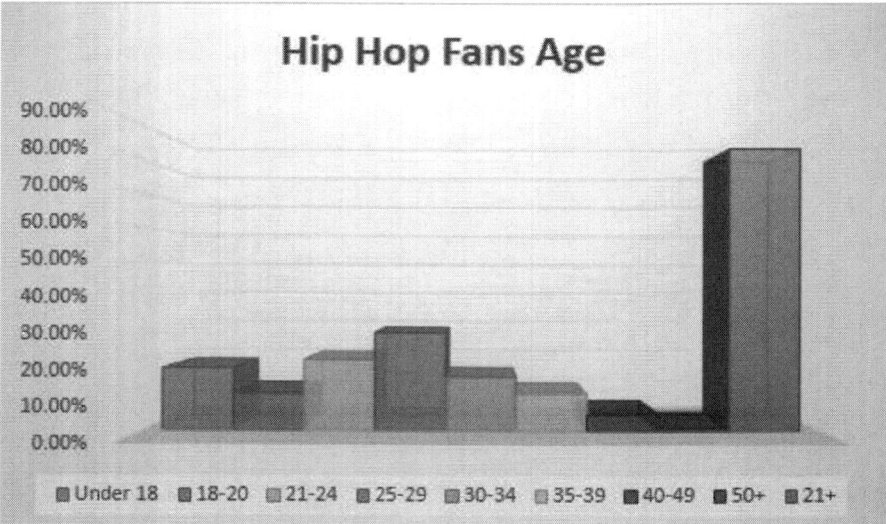

# Hip Hop Fans Median and Average Ages

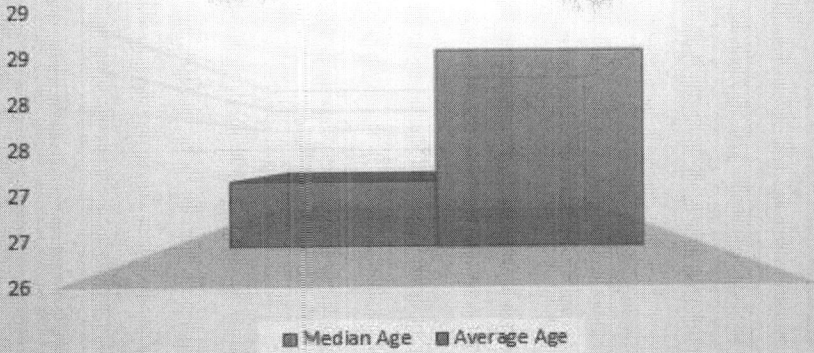

| | |
|---|---|
| 29 | |
| 29 | |
| 28 | |
| 28 | |
| 27 | |
| 27 | |
| 26 | |

■ Median Age   ■ Average Age

# Hip Hop Fans Ethnicity

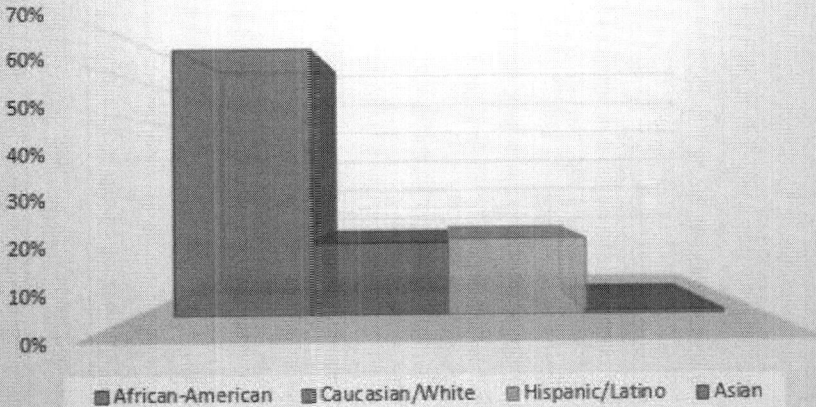

| | |
|---|---|
| 70% | |
| 60% | |
| 50% | |
| 40% | |
| 30% | |
| 20% | |
| 10% | |
| 0% | |

■ African-American   ■ Caucasian/White   ■ Hispanic/Latino   ■ Asian

# Hip Hop Fans Gender

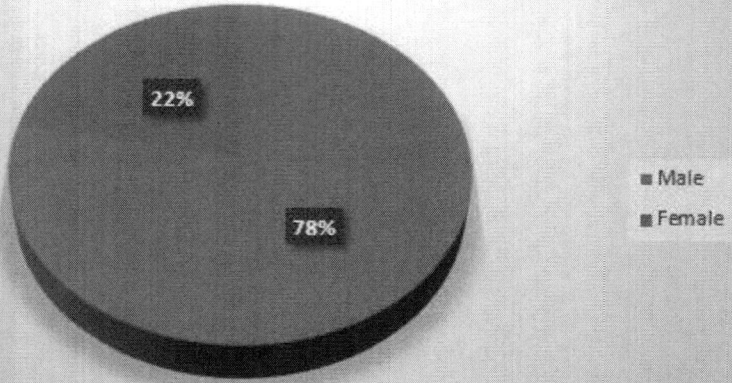

22%

78%

■ Male
■ Female

# Hip Hop Fans Income

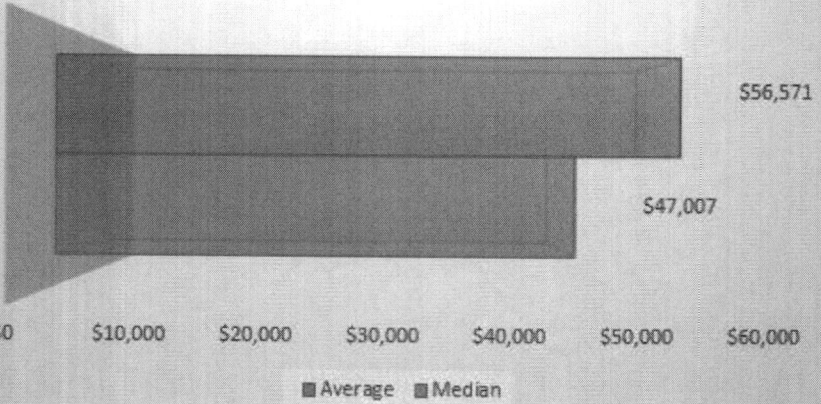

$56,571

$47,007

$0      $10,000     $20,000     $30,000     $40,000     $50,000     $60,000

■ Average  ■ Median

Sample Event Schedule

| | |
|---|---|
| April 11 – 13 | **Oschersleben (ADAC Masters Weekend)** |
| May 8 – 10 | **Assen (Netherlands) (ADAC Masters Weekend)** |
| May 22 – 24 | **Nurburgring (ADAC Zurich 24 Hours)** |
| June 5 – 7 | **Hockenheim (ADAC Masters Weekend)** |
| July 3 – 5 | **Lausitzring (ADAC Masters Weekend)** |
| August 21 – 23 | **Nurburgring (ADAC 1000km)** |
| September 18 – 20 | **Saschenring (ADAC Masters Weekend)** |
| October 16 – 18 | **Oschersleben (ADAC Masters Weekend)** |

**Finishing Touches**

To make sure the proposal looks great, you must do some simple things that every writer does with his finished work:

- Spell and Grammar check
- Prepare Table of Contents
- Prepare Cover Letter
- Prepare Section Tabs for the document (optional)
- Insert Special Pages and charts if applicable
- Check pages in each copy to make sure they are in the proper order

- Check each copy and make sure there are no missing pages
- Final reading of the document to spot any minor flaws and typographical errors
- Ask several people to read the proposal to make sure there are no flaws that you have missed

Most of the above can be done with your word processing software. It will ensure that you have dotted all the "i"s and crossed all the "t"s so to speak.

Now it is time to print it out, bind it and start sending it out. Good luck.

## About Document Services International

Document Services International specializes in the creation of high quality business documents including Business Plans, Sponsorship Proposals, Business Proposals, Internet Content, Ghostwriting, Resumes, Brochures and other business documents. We also specialize in graphic design and web design.

From our headquarters in Indianapolis, IN, we have created thousands of documents for authors, business startups, athletes, professional and amateur sports teams, entertainment professionals, concert promoters and sponsors from all over the world. Our document prices will help you make efficient use of your marketing dollars.

Business Plans and Sponsorship Proposals make up the bulk of our work. The company has written over 200 Business Plans and hundreds of Sponsorship Proposals. We are producing some of the best sponsorship proposals and business plans today.

www.documentservicesinternational.com
info@documentservicesinternational.com
Twitter: DSI2014
www.documentservicesinternational.com/books.html

About Robert Villegas

Robert Villegas is an Indiana Author specializing in fiction, romance, theater and philosophy. He was born in South Texas (Weslaco) but raised in Indiana. He is Hispanic-American but American in every sense of the word. He has spent a lifetime in the business world as a UPS executive and also worked in locations all over the United States and Europe. He is an Army veteran who served as a telecommunications specialist serving in the 7th Infantry Division in Camp Casey, Korea. He was educated in Indiana and earned a Degree through the University of the State of NY (Albany) via an external degree program. He is divorced with three grown children and three grandchildren.

www.robertvillegas.com

15509035R00030

Printed in Great Britain
by Amazon